VIOLA

CONTEMPORARY HITS

P9-DBN-127

HOW TO USE THE CD ACCOMPANIMENT:
A MELODY CUE APPEARS ON THE RIGHT CHANNEL ONLY. IF YOUR CD PLAYER HAS A BALANCE ADJUSTMENT, YOU CAN ADJUST THE VOLUME OF THE MELODY BY TURNING DOWN THE RIGHT CHANNEL.

ISBN 0-634-08535-2

HAL•LEONARD®
CORPORATION
7777 W. BLUEMOUND RD. P.O. BOX 13819 MILWAUKEE, WI 53213

Visit Hal Leonard Online at
www.halleonard.com

◆ ACCIDENTALLY IN LOVE

from the Motion Picture SHREK 2

VIOLA

Words and Music by ADAM DURITZ,
DAN VICKREY, DAVID IMMERGLUCK,
MATTHEW MALLEY and DAVID BRYSON

Moderately fast

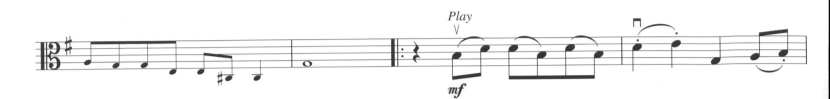

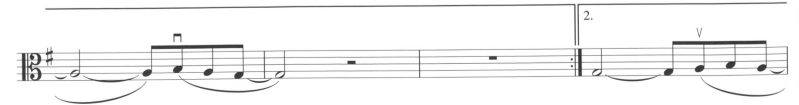

rit.

◆❷ CALLING ALL ANGELS

VIOLA

Words and Music by PAT MONAHAN,
SCOTT UNDERWOOD, JAMES STAFFORD
and CHARLIE COLIN

Moderately

5

◆ DON'T TELL ME

VIOLA

Words and Music by AVRIL LAVIGNE
and EVAN TAUBENFELD

◆ EVERYTHING

VIOLA

Words and Music by
ALANIS MORISSETTE

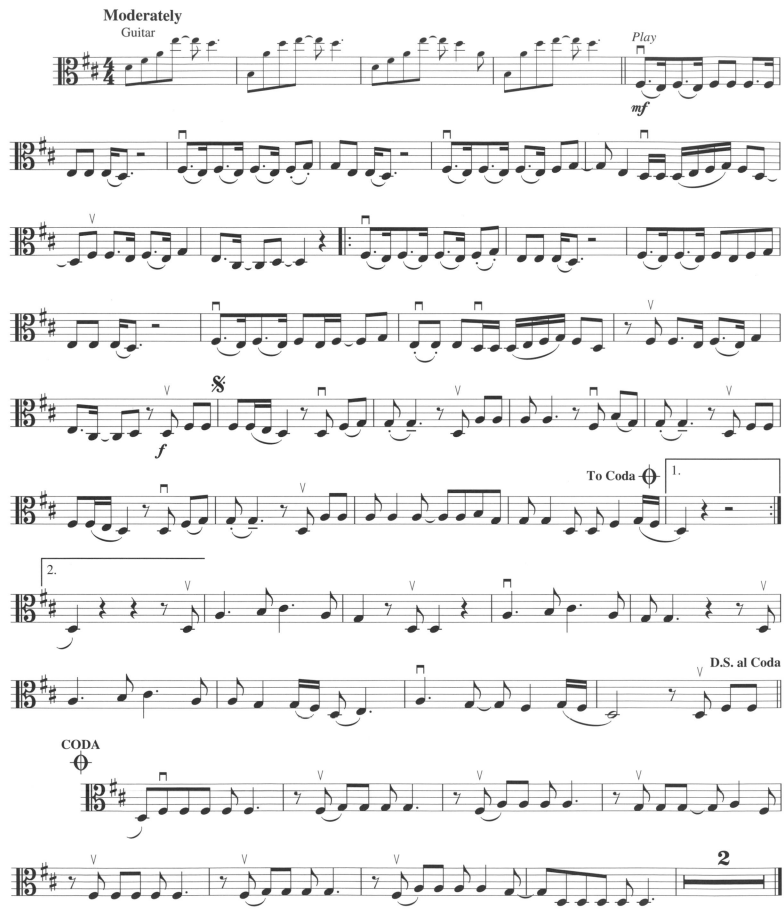

THE FIRST CUT IS THE DEEPEST

VIOLA

Words and Music by
CAT STEVENS

◆ FALLEN

VIOLA

Words and Music by
SARAH McLACHLAN

HERE WITHOUT YOU

Words and Music by BRAD ARNOLD,
MATTHEW DARRICK ROBERTS, CHRISTOPHER LEE HENDERSON
and ROBERT TODD HARRELL

VIOLA

◆ HEY YA!

VIOLA

Words and Music by
ANDRE BENJAMIN

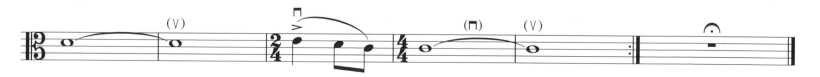

IF I AIN'T GOT YOU

VIOLA

Words and Music by
ALICIA KEYS

TAKE MY BREATH AWAY
(Love Theme)
from the Paramount Picture TOP GUN

VIOLA

Words and Music by GIORGIO MORODER
and TOM WHITLOCK

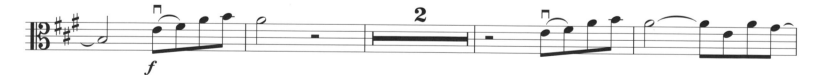

◆10 IT'S MY LIFE

VIOLA

Words and Music by MARK DAVID HOLLIS
and TIM FRIESE-GREENE

100 YEARS

VIOLA

Words and Music by
JOHN ONDRASIK

◆13 THIS LOVE

VIOLA

Words and Music by ADAM LEVINE
and JESSE CARMICHAEL

WHITE FLAG

VIOLA

Words and Music by RICK NOWELS,
ROLLO ARMSTRONG and DIDO ARMSTRONG

YOU RAISE ME UP

VIOLA

Words and Music by BRENDAN GRAHAM
and ROLF LOVLAND